# Our Love Story

Frederick and Talisha Belk were married at the tender age of nineteen (Frederick) and eighteen (Talisha). They began dating when Talisha was an eighth-grader in middle school, and Fred was a freshman in high school.  Even though they attended different high schools, they were able to continue their relationship with pure and genuine love.  The couple discussed marriage at a young age.  They understood the expectations of marriage because of their equally yoked upbringing. Their parents, nor the church, dictated those expectations – it was already in their hearts.

It seemed almost impossible to plan a wedding at such a young age.  Both had minimum wage jobs, and they were struggling to understand the real meaning of adulthood.

Routine Maintenance: Beyond the Vows
Copyright © 2020 by Frederick and Talisha Belk
All Rights Reserved

Although the author and publisher have made every effort to ensure that the information in this book was correct at press time, the author and publisher do not assume and hereby disclaim any liability to any party for any loss, damage, or disruption caused by errors or omissions, whether such errors or omissions result from negligence, accident, or any other cause. This book is not intended as a substitute for the medical advice of physicians or psychological advice from a licensed professional. The reader should regularly consult a physician in matters relating to his/her health and particularly with respect to any symptoms that may require diagnosis or medical attention or emotional status.

Publisher: **Absolute Author Publishing House**

Interior Designer: **DreamSeedsCreations**

Cover: **Alisia Berry (Custom Designs Lab)**

ISBN: **978-1-64953-009-7**

p. cm.

1. MARRIAGE  2. COUPLE'S THERAPY  3. SELF-HELP

# Preface

Please know that this is the companion book to the workbook, "His/Her Routine Maintenance" which should be used while reading this book. The workbook enhances the principles and tenets isolated in this book for further growth. The workbook encourages married couples with written assignments to explore scheduled maintenance on an ongoing basis to ensure a smooth ride and communication throughout their marriage and is available on Amazon.

However, they vowed to make it happen – one day. By faith, they went to the city offices, watched a movie on marriage, and filled out the paperwork. They had no idea how, or even when, they would get married.

Frederick and Talisha Belk were married at the tender age of nineteen (Frederick) and eighteen (Talisha). They began dating when Talisha was an eighth-grader in middle school, and Fred was a freshman in high school. Even though they attended different high schools, they were able to continue their relationship with pure and genuine love. The couple discussed marriage at a young age.

They understood the expectations of marriage because of their equally yoked upbringing. Their parents, nor the church, dictated those expectations – it was already in their hearts.

It seemed almost impossible to plan a wedding at such a young age. Both had minimum wage jobs, and they were struggling to understand the real meaning of adulthood. However, they vowed to make it happen – one day. By faith, they went to the city offices, watched a movie on marriage, and filled out the paperwork. They had no idea how, or even when, they would get married.

During a family reunion in 1994, the two sat together and affectionately engraved their names on a bench at their local park, Belle Isle.

On August 13, 1995, on that same bench, they were officially engaged. One month later, on the morning of Friday, September 15th, Fred called Talisha at work and asked, "Are we waiting for a specific date to get married?" Talisha paused and responded, "No." He then asked, "Well, what are we waiting for?" " immediately following up with, "I think we should just do it!" Talisha agreed and asked, "When?" "Today!" he said.

Talisha was surprised by Fred's response. Shocked, she began questioning the day. They decided to meet at City Hall on their lunch break. In their everyday work clothes, they walked into the courtroom with several other soon-to-be-married couples.

It was clear they were the youngest ones in the group that day. With such short notice, Antoinette Rucker (Fred's Mom), the judge performing the ceremony, and God were their witnesses. After the ceremony and the kiss, they headed back to work to finish out their day. In case you missed it – yes, they got married on their lunch break!

Talisha was surprised by Fred's response. Shocked, she began questioning the day. They decided to meet at City Hall on their lunch break. In their everyday work clothes, they walked into the courtroom with several other soon-to-be-married couples.

Questions and rumors started swirling around in the community. People were talking. They wondered why they would marry so young. The people whispered amongst themselves, "She must be pregnant." It was clear that most people didn't understand. Frederick and Talisha were destined to be together and wanted God to bless their union. Proverbs 18:22 (NIV) tells us he who finds a wife finds what is good and receives favor from the Lord. The two remained faithful to God and their first church home, First Fellowship Baptist Church. Fred found his wife, but they were still missing the favor of God. With much prayer, God's direction, and the blessing of their current Pastor, they obeyed the voice of the Lord.

In 2001 they joined Zion Hope Missionary Baptist Church, their next church home. They were preparing for the journey God had waiting for them.

After a devastating miscarriage in 2002, the Lord blessed Talisha and Fred with "double" for their trouble. In June 2003, Talisha gave birth to a healthy set of boy/girl twins. They named them Daniel and Danielle.

They continued to grow in God and ministry and accept God's call on their lives. In 2004, God directed the couple to start a marriage ministry in their home. The two decided to build the ministry on biblical principles and named it, "One Flesh Marriage Ministry".

They were able to minister to many couples right in their living room. As the ministry began to grow, their leader - Pastor Curtis R. Grant Jr. asked them to extend the ministry inside the church. To this day, Fred and Talisha are still committed to coaching couples prior to marriage and hosting sessions for "Routine Maintenance – Beyond the Vows".

In 2010, they both earned their Ministerial license to preach and teach the gospel of Christ. A few years later, Fred's parents unexpectedly passed within months of one another, but, in 2013, one day after Fred's mom went to be with the Lord, their daughter Chloe was born.

Fred and Talisha are confident she was an angel sent to provide peace and comfort after a horrific loss. God always provides a rainbow after the storm.

The call to lead came in August 2014. With disciplined training and following God's will, Frederick became the Pastor of his childhood church, Mount Charity Missionary Baptist Church. With prayer, obedience to God, and their Pastor's support, they took their ministry to another level. They were ordained together as Frederick took on the pastoral mantel. Frederick is still the proud Pastor of Mount Charity Missionary Baptist Church with Talisha working by his side.

In life and ministry, God has called them to work together. Throughout their journey, God has given them the passion and experience to mentor and coach married couples of all ages. Although it has not always been easy, they stand firm on their motto: God is the glue that has held us together throughout our journey.

# Dedication

We dedicate this book to Christ, the solid rock on which we stand. To our mother, the late Antoinette Coats who reminded us of the blessings of doing it "God's Way" & our Pastor and Father in ministry, Pastor Curtis R. Grant Jr.

*Marriage is not easy. Nowadays, it's easier to get out of a marriage than into one. We keep a record of one another's faults, clouding our own judgment and memory. We forget that our vows are not just to one another; they are unto God.*

God created man from dust (Genesis 2:7). When He created woman, it was more intimate and ordained: she was from his rib (Genesis 2:22), then they were one flesh (Genesis 2:24).

# Note from the Authors

While both of us come from broken homes, God has shown us a different way of life. We know that when we keep Him as the foundation of our marriage, we can break generational curses. God is the glue that has held us together through our ups and downs. He reminds us that what God put together, let no one put asunder (Matthew 19:6).

There is no perfect couple or marriage and every relationship goes through highs and lows. However, God provides strategies for maintaining a healthy relationship. When you feel you have mastered one part of your marriage, you will face challenges in other areas.

"Routine Maintenance" is essential for any relationship, and it's easy to do. Evaluate where you are in your marriage and what needs maintenance. Schedule an appointment to address your problems and figure out what you can improve. Remember, the longer you wait to fix your issues, the more you will pay for the repair.

# Contents

| | |
|---|---|
| Unrealistic Expectations | 1 |
| The Triangle Effect of Communication | 22 |
| Finances in Marriage | 34 |
| In-To-Me-I-See (Sex Signals) | 50 |
| Is It Grass or AstroTurf? | 71 |
| Stick – Stay – Pray | 82 |

# Unrealistic Expectations

# Maintenance Prayer

Heavenly Father we thank you for today. We thank you for your unconditional love towards us. We thank you that you've allowed us to come together in holy matrimony. God, we pray right now that you would give us an open heart and mind as we read this chapter. We recognize that neither of us are perfect and we can always take the time to make improvements or adjustments. Sometimes, we fear change but give us the strength and mindset to erase all the negativity. Change is good, change shows growth – anything that doesn't grow is considered dead and anything that is dead should be buried. God, we thank you that our marriage is not dead, and we are committed to our vows. God let us not have unrealistic expectations of one another, please remind us to use the triangle effect of communication and allow you to be our filter before addressing one another. God help us to discuss our finances and the decisions we need to make for our future. God, we know Intimacy can be hard to discuss, but let us continue to have conversations with respect, love, and consideration. Father remind us that the grass isn't greener on the other side but if we continue to care for one another and put in the work - we can bring our marriage back to a healthy state. Ultimately, God we thank you that we have one another; there are so many that desire to be married so we are grateful for the blessing of consistent companionship. When it's all said and done, God remind us that all things are possible through you and that we must stick, stay and pray through any adversity that comes against what you've ordained and put together.

In Jesus name we pray.....<br>
Amen

Before we talk about unrealistic expectations, we should first discuss how we got there. Unrealistic expectations come from both parties through our upbringing and other generational ideals. For instance, if you grew up in a two-parent home, your ideas about marriage and relationships may differ from those of someone who grew up in a single-parent home. Likewise, an individual raised by grandparents or other relatives may have a different viewpoint on marital relationships altogether. Outside sources can also impact the way we feel about marital bliss.

Most of us loved watching TV shows like The Brady Bunch and The Cosby Show. These families were the embodiment of perfection.

Additionally, the world has taught us the ingredients for an ideal family are a spouse, a white picket fence, two kids, and a dog. These scenarios are the gauge for "marital bliss." Still, they can also create misconceptions about the realities of the ideal union. Remember, you only see what each couple allows you to see. Outsiders usually are not privy to the ugly stuff. Misconceptions of the perfect marriage are why we have so many relationships with a ton of unrealistic expectations.

# Unrealistic Presumptions

We have expectations about our spouses, but they have no idea because these expectations are presumptions we've created. They are wish list items we place upon our relationship and talk about with friends. We say, "This is everything I want in a husband," or "these are all the things I want in a wife." We fixate on these ideas, but they're unrealistic because our partner is unaware of our expectations. One person can't be all the things we want them to be.

Many people jump into relationships or marriage with unrealistic expectations. When you first get involved with someone, you get butterflies in your stomach because you're excited about this new thing.

You're enthusiastic about getting to know him or her better. You don't know what their next move will be, what your next date will be like, and who they are during holidays or certain times of the year. The anticipation of being intimate with them makes you smile. These are the things you go through and the emotional rollercoaster you're on during the dating period.

When you first start dating, everything is bright, glorious, and beautiful. Your partner puts their best foot forward, and you love all the great things you're feeling. You daydream about your new love and form expectations about your future. You wonder if it will be a long-term relationship or a lifelong marriage.

You've got your "love blinders" on forgetting that the newness will get old, and the butterflies will fade. Impressing you is no longer at the top of their list.

You've disagreed on some issues, had your first argument, and you see him or her in a negative light. You realize your relationship is no longer rosy, and you can't help but wonder what happened. You haven't experienced how your new partner manages money, stress, or the loss of a loved one. It would help if you saw how they handle these things since this is the person you want to commit to for the **REST ... OF .... YOUR ... LIFE**.

We encourage our clients to stay with their partner for at least a year before getting married; and longer for couples in long-distance relationships.

Remember, people wear masks. A couple who spends all their time together may be ready to get married within three to six months or a year. On the other hand, the couple in a long-distance relationship, who only see each other four or five times a year, may need two or three years before they get married. They may not have seen their partner during the low points in life. These exceptions are why different circumstances justify divergent timelines.

The societal norms of long-term relationships have changed over the years. Many of us look for an exit on the way into the relationship. We have prenuptial agreements and divorce attorneys on speed dial. These are the things we think about as we get into the relationship. We tell ourselves, "If it doesn't work, I know I can get divorced because I've done it before. I can do it again. It's no problem." These thoughts are a critical problem. As we move forward with the relationship, we go in preparing our exit plan if it does not work out.

# Unrealistic Communication

Unrealistic expectations can stem from a lack of communication. You think to yourself, "How am I supposed to know what you expect from me if you haven't told me?" Changes will continue to happen throughout your marriage. When you don't communicate with your partner, you base your actions on outdated information. Maintaining constant communication circumvents misunderstandings within the relationship. The understanding and knowledge of what you want and need from each other emanate through open communication.

Over the years, as your relationship grows, you change and your expectations of one another change.

It's unrealistic to expect your partner to reach into your mind and figure out what is different. It is helpful when you can express those changes constructively, so you may need to get creative with your methods of communication. If you need to see a therapist regularly to define clear expectations and monitor changes, do it. These are the times when you must live your vows – till death do us part.

One misconception about relationships is that we only need to seek counsel when things have hit rock bottom. That's one of the main reasons we talk about routine maintenance in our relationships. Like your car, you can't wait until things start falling apart before getting regular maintenance. If you change the oil regularly, your vehicle will last for years; but if you wait until you hear knocking, you've blown a rod. If you blow a rod, it doesn't mean it's not repairable. It just means the mechanic who could do the oil change may not be qualified to replace the engine or repair the rod. Seeking an engine replacement from a person who's training is only to change oil is a common mistake.

When you make the mistake of bringing your blown rod to the oil change mechanic, you run the risk of making the problem worse. They don't know what to do with you or your situation. They could have handled your issue if there was a regular schedule of maintenance. Since there wasn't, you now have a bigger problem. Regular maintenance alleviates confusion. Do you know those quick lube places where they only change the oil? Those mechanics don't know how to change a blown rod because they are not qualified. Now you have to find a specialist who knows how to do that type of work.

When you're in a relationship, you can't afford to skip routine maintenance checkups. Regular maintenance, although not mandatory, is highly recommended.

Discussing issues or concerns before they become significant problems is healthy. Even when you feel your marriage is running smoothly, you can always learn your spouse's needs – remember, they may have changed. Routine maintenance communication sessions are an excellent time to discuss short term goals, house projects, vacation ideas, or the children's future, among other things.

Unfortunately, some people have the propensity to go to the wrong people for counseling and coaching. The bible warns us of ungodly counsel. The person you discuss your problems with could be the difference between your relationship's success or failure.

While it's easy to vent to a friend, parent, or family member, you must ask yourself: "Can this person help my current situation?" After you have vented and spilled the beans, all you receive is a biased opinion from someone who loves you.

Since people habitually place unrealistic expectations on each other, we want to talk to you about counseling and coaching.

The decision to see a professional is a big deal. It's important to continue routine maintenance because you can always talk about your expectations with one another. Unfortunately, because we place unrealistic expectations upon our partner, we put additional pressure on them. We expect our partner to be our peace instead of the God we serve.

We expect our partner to be our peace instead of the God we serve. These actions cause negative thoughts. Then, we believe and say, "You're no longer my peace, and I don't want to be in a relationship with you anymore." You must understand that you are causing more chaos with these thoughts. Ultimately, in some cases, we divorce people because we expect them to be what God should be.

We want you to know that it is okay to seek outside help. You'll get an unbiased opinion from a person committed to the relationship, not to one person or the other. Be warned, though – most people won't tell you when they're unqualified to deal with specific issues.

How many would tell you they're not qualified to handle your problem? Most would not.

That oil change mechanic will take your engine replacement money and say, "I can handle it." So, be careful. Don't bring your complex problems to a less qualified professional. Whether you seek help from a spiritual counselor or a nonspiritual counselor, ascertain the counselor's qualifications.

Finally, the most common unrealistic expectation in the relationship is the expectation of never-ending happiness. You'll say, "Because you made me happy before the marriage, I expect you to make me happy throughout the marriage."

You look to that individual to define your happiness. God should be the only one who makes you happy and be the source of your joy. When you have that happiness within yourself, you can then create happiness around you.

*House of Harmony.*

When we get home from a hard day at work, we want to relax. Sometimes when we get there, chaos lurks around the corner. We have unrealistic expectations that our spouse, family, and kids are supposed to create happiness when we walk through the door. In addition to the everyday stress, we put that pressure on our spouse as well. "You're the one who should be making me happy. You should be my peace. I should be able to come to you, and you make me feel better." That's just too big of a hat to lay on your spouse.

That is the hat that God should wear. That is the place and the space that God should reside.

Designate your home as the House of Peace. Use your alone time for reflection, dedication, and prayer. If you pray on your way home, or when you're by yourself, you become the peace.

When you're in God and God is in you, if you take that time to pray, meditate, and evaluate how good God has been to you, you can change the atmosphere and become the peace when you get home. Take inventory, start building your peace, and say:

I thank you God for a job

I thank you God for my spouse

I thank you God for my kids

I thank you God for all the blessings you've given me

This is the day that You have made

I will rejoice and be glad in it

# The Triangle Effect of Communication

# Maintenance Prayer

Heavenly Father we thank you for today. We thank you for your unconditional love towards us. We thank you that you've allowed us to come together in holy matrimony. God, we pray right now that you would give us an open heart and mind as we read this chapter. We recognize that neither of us are perfect and we can always take the time to make improvements or adjustments. Sometimes, we fear change but give us the strength and mindset to erase all the negativity. Change is good, change shows growth – anything that doesn't grow is considered dead and anything that is dead should be buried. God, we thank you that our marriage is not dead, and we are committed to our vows. God let us not have unrealistic expectations of one another, please remind us to use the triangle effect of communication and allow you to be our filter before addressing one another. God help us to discuss our finances and the decisions we need to make for our future. God, we know Intimacy can be hard to discuss, but let us continue to have conversations with respect, love, and consideration. Father remind us that the grass isn't greener on the other side but if we continue to care for one another and put in the work – we can bring our marriage back to a healthy state. Ultimately, God we thank you that we have one another; there are so many that desire to be married so we are grateful for the blessing of consistent companionship. When it's all said and done, God remind us that all things are possible through you and that we must stick, stay and pray through any adversity that comes against what you've ordained and put together.

In Jesus name we pray.....
Amen

Moreover if thy brother shall trespass against thee, go and tell him his fault between thee and him alone: if he shall hear thee, thou hast gained thy brother. But if he will not hear thee, then take with thee one or two more, that in the mouth of two or three witnesses every word may be established. And if he shall neglect to hear them, tell it unto the church: but if he neglect to hear the church, let him be unto thee as an heathen man and a publican. *(Matthew 18:15-17 KJV)*

*Fret not about anything, but in everything, by prayer and supplication, let your request be known unto God.*
*- (Philippians 4:6 KJV)*

*Wherefore, my beloved brethren, let every man be swift to hear and slow to speak, slow to wrath.*
*- (James 1:19 KJV)*

Numbers don't lie. The stats show that sex, finances, and communication are the three key factors driving marriage toward divorce.[1] It is difficult to have sex or discuss finances when communication is ineffective or nonexistent. Ineffective communication can result in unnecessary arguments, hurtful comments, and eventually cause division. Communication is the key to a healthy marriage.

The Bible tells us we need to talk to Him to resolve issues. Sex, money, and communication can gauge the health of a marriage. To help maintain a healthy marriage, we have developed a useful three-sided tool. In fact, it looks like a triangle. We call this tool the Triangle Effect of Communication. The points of the triangle are incredibly important. The top peak represents God, and the right and left sides represent you and your spouse.

---

[1] https://www.marriage.com/advice/divorce/10-most-common-reasons-for-divorce/

Every marriage should consult God first and follow His direction on how to resolve issues. He will tell you to leave it alone and let Him handle it. He will tell you to keep it to yourself – for now. Sometimes, He will give you permission to discuss the problem with your spouse. Just remember, no matter how nice you put it, or how much honey you put on it, some issues will cause an argument or a notable disagreement. You will discover that once you let that thought or comment come out of your mouth, there's no turning back!

Some people find it necessary to blurt out whatever is on their mind.

Ask yourself this question: do you tend to say it when you're irritated by the very issue you're trying to talk about? If so, how do you really think it's going to turn out? That's why we believe you should first ask God if the time is right to speak with your spouse about the issues that are bothering you.

If all you do is complain, your spouse may feel their efforts to please you are in vain. We often talk about the 20% of your relationship that you always want to change. We grabbed this concept from the movie Why Did I Get Married?[2] where they talk about the "80/20 Rule."[3]

---

[2] Bobb, R. (Producer), Perry T. (Director). (2007). Why did I get married? [Motion Picture]. United States: Lionsgate.
[3] https://www.youtube.com/watch?v=Wcd2haXsCPk

The rule says you're never satisfied with 20% of your spouse at any given time, and there's always something that you want to change about them. Even if you create your list now, and they change everything you put on there, by the time they have worked through your list, mentally you will have made a completely new list.

The Bible says the flesh is never satisfied (Proverbs 27:20). You never want your spouse to feel as though their efforts are useless and can't meet your needs.

We believe in applauding their efforts. They may not do everything you imagined they would do. They may not do everything you imagined they would do.

Still, the fact that they're doing something helps you realize they are listening to your concerns and love you enough to address them. People typically wait until the relationship is in disrepair. Then they call for coaching or counseling as a last resort just to be able to say, "I tried." By this time, the relationship is at the point of no return. Learn how to do small exercises early on to help your communication rather than wait until it's too late.

When talking to God about how much you want your spouse to change, be careful because God will show you your mistakes and shortcomings, and how you can do better! Many times, we selfishly think of what the other person should and could do for us, but what have you done for them lately? Please realize that you are not perfect, and neither are they.

The Bible says if we say that we have no sin, we deceive ourselves, and the truth is not in us (1 John 1:8). So many of us spend all day pointing the finger at the other that we never really sit down and allow God to show us our faults! Ask yourself this question: what can you do better?

Excellent communication goes a long way! We do an exercise where we ask the other, "What are five things you would like me to change?"

We believe this exercise should be done at least once a year. You can find this activity in our Routine Maintenance workbook. It opens the door to address concerns that irritate you, without expressing them in frustration. Most of the time, the request is small and highly achievable. We call this the "Routine Maintenance" check. This is when you check to see if everything is alright in the relationship.

Do not do this exercise when you're frustrated. It will not work.

The Routine Maintenance check, in your relationship, is equivalent to listening for engine knocks and maintaining regular oil changes on your vehicle. If you are the type of person who listens to your car, you don't wait until you hear the engine knocking to get an oil change. You take it for service to get a routine maintenance check. If you wait until the engine is knocking, you will pay more to fix the problem. You will also learn that only a select number of professionals can handle your exacerbated problem. Remember, there's a higher percentage of people who can address simple problems. The Routine Maintenance check allows you to determine if there are any significant issues on the horizon and fix small problems while they are still small enough to manage.

*The Triangle Effect of Communication*

# Finances in Marriage

# Maintenance Prayer

Heavenly Father we thank you for today. We thank you for your unconditional love towards us. We thank you that you've allowed us to come together in holy matrimony. God, we pray right now that you would give us an open heart and mind as we read this chapter. We recognize that neither of us are perfect and we can always take the time to make improvements or adjustments. Sometimes, we fear change but give us the strength and mindset to erase all the negativity. Change is good, change shows growth – anything that doesn't grow is considered dead and anything that is dead should be buried. God, we thank you that our marriage is not dead, and we are committed to our vows. God let us not have unrealistic expectations of one another, please remind us to use the triangle effect of communication and allow you to be our filter before addressing one another. God help us to discuss our finances and the decisions we need to make for our future. God, we know Intimacy can be hard to discuss, but let us continue to have conversations with respect, love, and consideration. Father remind us that the grass isn't greener on the other side but if we continue to care for one another and put in the work - we can bring our marriage back to a healthy state. Ultimately, God we thank you that we have one another; there are so many that desire to be married so we are grateful for the blessing of consistent companionship. When it's all said and done, God remind us that all things are possible through you and that we must stick, stay and pray through any adversity that comes against what you've ordained and put together.

In Jesus name we pray.....<br>
Amen

# Going into the Marriage in Debt

When we talk about the wedding ceremony and all the fanfare that comes with it, we have a problem with couples who bite off more than they can chew. The wedding, the reception, the honeymoon, the ring. All these things cause them to go into the marriage in debt. This can cause financial stress to an already stressful situation. Communication, finances, and sex are the primary causes of divorce. Financial problems often begin when couples try to impress other people. Sadly, these are the same people who do not really care whether our relationship succeeds or fails. We encourage you to only do what you can afford.

Over 60% of newlyweds start their marriage indebted to creditors, and 73% regret their decision.[4] Remember, debt equals stress.

---

[4] https://cdn.ramseysolutions.net/media/b2c/personalities/rachel/PR/MoneyMarriageAndCommunication.pdf?_ga=2.85960987.360093093.1595097863-519153239.1594662057

# Know Your Budget

When I was 19 and my wife was 18, we married at our hometown City Council office. We were in love, and we knew we wanted to be together forever. We had a no-frills ceremony because that was our budget. Twenty years later when we reviewed our budget, we had our dream wedding, and a great honeymoon. It was a great way to celebrate our 20th Anniversary. We loved it because we stuck to our budget. We did not go into too much debt, and we felt great about our decisions.

Please understand, the girl who married me in front of the judge was the 18-year old Talisha. The 25 or 30-year old Talisha may not have allowed us to simply go to the City Council building, on our lunch break, and get married

It was a great benefit to us that we did not start our marriage in debt. There is a special kind of stress on the relationship's finances if you are two, three, four, even five years into the marriage and still paying for the wedding. So, to get to the core issue of your financial problems, you may have to acknowledge that you spent more on the wedding than you should have.

Traditionally, wedding costs used to fall on the bride and groom's parents, and the sky was the limit. The weddings were lavish because "Aunt Susie can't know we're really broke." Nowadays, many couples cover their own costs, but they still have the same dilemma: cash or credit. There is nothing wrong with a ceremony that has all the bells and whistles. Matching the desire with the budget is the problem. When you know your budget, you know what you can spend.

In some cultures, the family ensures the gifts can cover the deposit on a new home. We need to think about that. You must know your budget. According to a 2018 Fidelity Investments study, 67% of couples concerned about debt admitted they argued more about money versus the 41% who were not concerned about their creditors. In that same study,[5] 46% agreed that money is the biggest challenge in their relationship. On the other hand, 16% of couples who did not have debt issues did not have many arguments about money. You must know your budget.

If you know you will receive $20,000 in gifts, then you know you can spend $20,000 for your ceremony, and not go into the marriage with debt. On the other hand, the average couple never enjoys that return on their investment. If you know you won't receive monetary gifts from your guests, you should not spend a ton of money for your ceremony.

---

[5] https://www.fidelity.com/bin-public/060_www_fidelity_com/documents/pr/couples-fact-sheet.pdf

# You Have the Power

Women generally rule the wedding budget. The groom typically does not care about the ceremony or the reception. He's focusing on making his future wife happy. If you want to go to the justice of the peace, then do it. As a couple, you must do what is right for you. If you decide to spend beyond your means, then none of it matters because you're stuck with all the bills and a lot of debt once you have spent your money. Review your finances and determine what you can afford. If you want your marriage to succeed, do not go into it in debt. Seven out of ten young couples who created wedding debt felt the debt had a 46% negative impact on the relationship.

# Let's Talk About It

After the wedding, hot topics include buying a house, kids' college funds, and retirement. Every relationship is different. Whether you already have children or blending a family, you guys must figure out who you owe. This includes child support, credit cards, and the storage unit. All these things can put stress on the relationship but must be part of the discussion. Conflict about money is the number one reason couples argue, and the number two reason they get divorced.[7] If a couple can find mutual ground with their finances, the marriage will likely succeed. There is no cookie-cutter way that marriage works, but couples can do things to increase their chances of success. Communication is vital, and sharing the burden is fair.

---

[7] https://www.daveramsey.com/blog/the-truth-about-money-and-relationships

The household budget should be freely discussed and agreed to by both parties. In nine out of ten relationships, one spouse is more financially adept and more familiar with the monthly bills. Some families split the bills down the middle, and others divide them up based on salary. There are different ways to handle finances. The approach you take will depend on your needs and preferences. You need to know your budget. You should know where you stand financially, and you should know which creditors you owe. You can create spreadsheets to track this info.

# The Responsibility Game

Sometimes one person has more knowledge about finances and budgeting. That does not mean everything should be left up to that individual. Leaving the responsibility entirely on one spouse, including those tough decisions, may cause more resistance from the less dominant spouse. No matter how much a person dominates the household finances, both parties need to be involved with the financial decisions. One study found that 80% of women handle their own finances because of unforeseen circumstances. Almost 60% regretted not taking a greater interest in the household finances during their marriage.[8]

---

[8] https://money.cnn.com/2018/05/29/pf/women-finances-husbands-ubs-report/index.html

On the other hand, one person feels it is their responsibility to bring home the money, and the other person's duty to pay the bills. They earn the money, slap it on the table, deposit it in the account, and their spouse pays the bills. This cycle becomes a problem because the person bringing home the money does not know how the other person is spending "their" money. Now they feel like they have nothing to show for the money they earned. Male or female, the question remains the same: "Where's my money?" Couples should sit down, talk about their finances, work with one another, and make decisions together. People in healthy relationships communicate regularly (54%) about money matters compared to those in unhealthy relationships (29%).[9]

---

[8] https://money.cnn.com/2018/05/29/pf/women-finances-husbands-ubs-report/index.html
[9] https://www.daveramsey.com/blog/the-truth-about-money-and-relationships

The financial burden is the responsibility of the couple, not one person or the other. From the car note, the mortgage, and the insurance, every bill belongs to both of you. These are your creditors too. When figuring out the finances, if the responsibility falls on one person, it can be incredibly stressful. That person is tasked with calling creditors and making payment arrangements on their own. It is not fair. Avoid this problem and share the responsibility. When asked which person primarily handled the finances, 30% of men said they did, and 23% of women said it was on them.[10]

---

[10] https://www.fidelity.com/bin-public/060_www_fidelity_com/documents/pr/couples-fact-sheet.pdf

# Big-Ticket Debt Commitment

Buying a house, a car, or returning to school are big-ticket decisions. These are matters you should discuss together because these purchases place added financial stress on the relationship. You will need to allocate more money from your monthly budget to meet your new payment obligation. Even if you buy something outright, you should still discuss the purchase with your spouse – even if it is a brand-new car. Perhaps a pushy salesperson pressured you into making the purchase. Stop them and say, "I need to talk to my spouse." Remember, you will not only have to pay the car note, but you will also be responsible for the insurance, gas, and maintenance.

Some people feel they have the right to purchase anything they want because they are the sole or primary breadwinner. They do not care if it's a car, a bigger house, or a dog. This is a problem because anything can happen. If you're a business owner, your business could go belly-up, or slow down. If you work a 9-5, you could get laid off or lose your job. Many things could happen during your marriage. Don't be cocky about your ability to make these purchases on your own. You never know if the tables will turn, forcing your spouse to take responsibility for the debts you committed to on your own.

# The Takeaway

Communication is key. Create your budget and discuss your finances. These talks may frighten you but go for it because they will strengthen your relationship.

# In-To-Me-I-See
## (Sex Signals)

# Maintenance Prayer

Heavenly Father we thank you for today. We thank you for your unconditional love towards us. We thank you that you've allowed us to come together in holy matrimony. God, we pray right now that you would give us an open heart and mind as we read this chapter. We recognize that neither of us are perfect and we can always take the time to make improvements or adjustments. Sometimes, we fear change but give us the strength and mindset to erase all the negativity. Change is good, change shows growth - anything that doesn't grow is considered dead and anything that is dead should be buried. God, we thank you that our marriage is not dead, and we are committed to our vows. God let us not have unrealistic expectations of one another, please remind us to use the triangle effect of communication and allow you to be our filter before addressing one another. God help us to discuss our finances and the decisions we need to make for our future. God, we know Intimacy can be hard to discuss, but let us continue to have conversations with respect, love, and consideration. Father remind us that the grass isn't greener on the other side but if we continue to care for one another and put in the work - we can bring our marriage back to a healthy state. Ultimately, God we thank you that we have one another; there are so many that desire to be married so we are grateful for the blessing of consistent companionship. When it's all said and done, God remind us that all things are possible through you and that we must stick, stay and pray through any adversity that comes against what you've ordained and put together.

In Jesus name we pray.....<br>Amen

Sexual fantasies are normal, and we get excited when we think about them. There is nothing more satisfying or sexually fulfilling than when your partner connects with you mentally and physically. We enjoy it when those fantasies play out in the bedroom. Sometimes we share them with our spouse, and sometimes we don't. When we don't express our sexual wants and needs, or take the time to learn our partner's sexual likes and dislikes, problems intensify and lead to uneasiness and divorce. Let's talk about some of the undisclosed secrets lingering under the sheets that cause friction in marriages. [11] [12]

---

[11] https://money.cnn.com/2018/05/29/pf/women-finances-husbands-ubs-report/index.html
[12] https://www.daveramsey.com/blog/the-truth-about-money-and-relationships

# Signals Crossed

We want to address this topic from the perspective of our actions when we get into premarital relationships. During this time, sex is non-stop – just like a green light. We do it all the time. We're adventurous with our sexual appetite and open to all sorts of things. You know what we mean. We put on costumes, risqué outfits, and, as we would say, hang from the chandelier. On the other hand, when we get married, we stop the carefree sexual exploits, and act as though we've been stopped by a red light. If this sounds familiar, your signals are crossed.

From a routine maintenance standpoint, couples need to talk about these crossed signals. You must first acknowledge that the intimacy between you and your spouse has slowed down. Talking about this sensitive subject may be one of the problems that couples deal with when it comes to sex. So, before we get into anything else, we want to tell you that it's time to change the signal. It is time to change that light from red to green.

It's okay to talk about sex, whether it's good or bad. During our client counseling sessions, we've learned that married couples do not talk about sex.

They don't talk about what they like, nor do they talk about what they expect. This lack of communication is a problem because sexual expectations change. If you're like us and married at a young age, your sexual expectations might be higher than other couples. You might think five to seven times per week is good. As your life changes and you grow in your marriage, you begin to realize that the regular schedule is unrealistic. So, it's okay to talk about it. You will have to do it continuously because things change, your lives change, and your circumstances change. Remember, it's not taboo to talk about sex in marriage. Sex is what we should be talking about.

Marriage is also about compromise. How can you compromise if you don't know the expectations? You may want sex three times per week, and your husband may want it five.

Hopefully, you can compromise and agree on four. Who knows? You might get a little spontaneous one morning – and he just got his five.

Women are emotional, and men are physical. People don't understand these differences. To get to a woman's body, you must bond with her emotionally. During our counseling sessions over the last 15 years, we have continued to tell our male clients, that the path to their wife's body is through her mind.

It's best if you make her feel good about herself. Even though you're married, whatever you did to get her is what it will take to keep her.

Some men are under the misconception that he only needs to date or court his wife once. They tell themselves, "I did that to get her, and now I don't need to do it anymore." They jump into bed, expecting illuminated candles and a disco ball hanging from the ceiling. Those things don't happen because you haven't reached her emotional core to get her to that place.

Sometimes a sweet text message in the middle of the day can soften her heart and put her in the mood. Small gestures work wonders. These seemingly insignificant actions bring us back to communication and expectations.

Remember, communication, finances, and sex are the top three reasons for divorce. Without communication, you can't have satisfying sex or fix your finances. When engaging with your woman, communication is the critical component. The way to her mind is through communication. You must continuously learn what she likes in bed so that your sexual relationship can evolve.

As women, we must understand that men are physical. In the same way we want them to understand our emotional side, we must respect their physical side. We can't make them feel what we feel, nor can we force them to understand what it takes to prepare our minds for intimacy. We talk about In-To-Me-I-See, which is a part of preparing a woman's mind for intimacy. If our goal is to make one another happy during sex, we must first engage in self-reflection. If we are both focused on making one another happy, then we will both be satisfied sexually. Still, we cannot please one another without talking to, and understanding, each other. We know what men want, what they like, and we should know what pleases our man.

Since he is physical in nature, sometimes we need to succumb to his physical needs. The way we want to experience the emotional part of intimacy is the same way he wants the physical side of intimacy. If we are honest with ourselves, we know the emotional connection is not always there. Sometimes we need to be physical without the mind games. Unfortunately, as women, we make our spouses jump through hoops when it comes to sex. As women, we should learn to let our guard down, get past our feelings, and realize that sometimes our husbands need physical intimacy. [13][14][15][16][17]

---

[13] https://www.verywellmind.com/giving-cheating-spouse-second-chance-2303074

[14] https://www.lifehack.org/articles/communication/10-ways-prevent-cheating-relationship.html

[15] https://www.theglobeandmail.com/life/relationships/the-truth-about-infidelity-why-researchers-say-its-time-to-rethink-cheating/article28717694/

[16] https://www.zurinstitute.com/infidelity/

[17] https://hernorm.com/infidelity-statistics/#:~:text=According%20to%20the%20infidelity%20statistics,sometime%20during%20their%20marital%20life.

# Sex Signals

Sex signals can make or break the moment. Now that you've talked about what you like, how you want it, and when you desire it, we need to discuss your timing and delivery of sex signal messages. Please be sure to use the accompanying Workbooks to start this and more conversations. It is a complete turn off when you're in the middle of being intimate, and one person doesn't like something the other person has said or done. Developing sex signals is prudent so that your moment is not spoiled. Many couples have arguments about a ruined night, a missed opportunity, or the inability to connect with their spouse.

During your intimate moments, there may be something your partner introduces that you do not like. Instead of giving them an outright "No!" or getting up and storming off, you must set up sex signals. If you don't, you run the risk of turning off your spouse and ruining the moment. I realize it's a big thing with comedians and the pineapple joke, but they are onto something. You must come up with sex signals when, without being rude, you feel the need to stop the action, letting your partner know this is not a good idea tonight, and I don't want to do that. There is a sweet loving way you can get your message across. It could be a gesture, a saying, or a nudge. Sex signals enable you to be intimate in a way that does not turn off your spouse.

Honesty can flow between you while letting your spouse know that what they are doing does not work for you.

When exploring new things sexually, there may be things you enjoy that do not please your spouse. Sex signals allow you to explore new ideas comfortably. Instead of abruptly saying, "Oh, I don't like that," he or she can sensually grab your ear or arm, or lightly tap your leg. These are examples of sex signals that will help intimacy continue without hard feelings. Lots of couples miss the opportunity to enhance or explore their desires because of rude or abrupt denials. Their response can destroy the moment, causing the giver to become frustrated and upset. Avoid the problem and develop your own set of sex signals.

# P-Punishment

The P represents either P-word, but we are talking about putting each other on sex punishment. You know what we're talking about here. When you're mad at your spouse, and you put him or her on punishment and say, "Oh no, you can't have this because I'm mad at you."

Take a dog, for example. An innocent dog can turn vicious if you starve it. P-Punishment is the same thing. Be careful about neglecting an area of your marriage that can be satisfied somewhere else. You can push your spouse into the arms of another person, pornography, or an alternative lifestyle.

These are things they should not have to deal with in the relationship. P-Punishment is not wise. As marriage coaches, we advise our clients never to put their spouse on P-Punishment.

Suppose there is an issue between you, and the only way you can get your point across is to put your spouse on P-Punishment.

If that's the case, you are not playing fair or respecting your relationship. The Bible says you should not let the sun go down on your wrath (Ephesians 4:26 KJV). This means you should not allow the day to go by without fixing your outstanding issues and problems.

Realistically, we understand that sometimes the sun does go down because one of you may be banished from the bedroom and forced to sleep on the couch, but that should not be your goal. Your goal should be not to let the sun go down without fixing the problem. If, as we said, your husband is physical, sometimes that is where the best makeup sex comes into play. All the muck gets thrown on the back burner or even eliminated because you have made up. You are physical, which can resolve some of the disagreements.

# It's a Bedroom, Not a PornHub

Porn is a sensitive subject but makes for a meaningful conversation. Unfortunately, this curse plagues a lot of men. As a young man, you may have been introduced to porn by a trusted adult, creating a hunger for pornography-style sex. Today, technology gives us a front-row seat to all kinds of fetishes. With this type of access, many married men enjoy watching porn. This habit can eventually turn the marital bed into a porn hub because we try to bring pornography into our bedroom. I'm sure you've watched porn without your spouse and tried something new that she did not enjoy. Did your feelings get hurt when she turned you down? If you want to spice up the relationship and try something new, talk about it first.

Honest communication could get your spouse's buy-in and get her on board. Use your sex signals so you can explore new things. Don't be disappointed if your wholesome wife doesn't enjoy sex like a porn star. We always say, "You can't turn a whore into a housewife." However, no one talks about how difficult it is to turn your housewife into a whore.

Some couples use toys to spice up the relationship. These can be dangerous because using them can hinder a woman from naturally reaching her climax.
In addition to new moves and toys, more couples are having threesomes. When we talk about the dangers of jumping into certain things, this is a prime example of what we mean.

We've had a couple of cases where the wife, because of the threesome, began wanting women more than she wanted to be with her man. These women turned to a lesbian lifestyle because they were introduced to the threesome by their husbands.

The Bible says the bedroom is undefiled *(Hebrews 13:4 KJV)*. Bringing another woman (or man) into your bedroom is adultery. It doesn't matter if you have mutual consent. In the sight of God, it is still adultery. Just because somebody tells you it's okay to steal, doesn't mean it's okay to become a thief. Be aware of what you do. Be careful about what you bring into your bedroom. Some spirits come with those decisions, and you must deal with the challenge of getting rid of them.[18]

---

[18] Undefiled is defined as not made corrupt, impure, or unclean. (https://www.merriam-webster.com/dictionary/undefiled)

# Be Glad

Talk about sex. We realize it's scary. The Workbooks will help you start these conversations. There's no cookie-cutter plan we can outline for you. The choice is yours. Talk about how you like it and when you want it. Share your fantasies. Throw around ideas and test them out. Explore new positions. Establish intimate boundaries. Most of all, have fun. Remember, In-To-Me-I-See opens intimacy.

# Is It Grass or AstroTurf?

# Maintenance Prayer

Heavenly Father we thank you for today. We thank you for your unconditional love towards us. We thank you that you've allowed us to come together in holy matrimony. God, we pray right now that you would give us an open heart and mind as we read this chapter. We recognize that neither of us are perfect and we can always take the time to make improvements or adjustments. Sometimes, we fear change but give us the strength and mindset to erase all the negativity. Change is good, change shows growth – anything that doesn't grow is considered dead and anything that is dead should be buried. God, we thank you that our marriage is not dead, and we are committed to our vows. God let us not have unrealistic expectations of one another, please remind us to use the triangle effect of communication and allow you to be our filter before addressing one another. God help us to discuss our finances and the decisions we need to make for our future. God, we know Intimacy can be hard to discuss, but let us continue to have conversations with respect, love, and consideration. Father remind us that the grass isn't greener on the other side but if we continue to care for one another and put in the work - we can bring our marriage back to a healthy state. Ultimately, God we thank you that we have one another; there are so many that desire to be married so we are grateful for the blessing of consistent companionship. When it's all said and done, God remind us that all things are possible through you and that we must stick, stay and pray through any adversity that comes against what you've ordained and put together.

                    In Jesus name we pray…..
                          Amen

It's not uncommon to question the choices we make in our relationships. We are agitated by what's in front of us, so we look at other options around us. We subliminally compare ourselves to other people, sometimes envying who they are or the how "good" their relationship looks from the outside. In turn, these feelings force us to ask ourselves, "Am I with the right person?"

*Temptation comes from desires, which entice us and drag us away.*
*- James 1:14 NLT*

We should be careful not to covet someone else's relationship or the things our parents showed us growing up. You must realize that you are not your parents or any other relationship you've been around. You are developing your relationship. We live in a world where we are mesmerized by the images we see on social outlets, TV, and movies. We start to believe the false realities of celebrities and social media influencers. These images play a role in our belief that the grass is greener on the other side. The Bible reminds us that we are never tempted by things that we would not already have a desire for (James 1:14).

It's easy to focus on what your spouse does wrong. However, marriages will last longer if we concentrate on the positive aspects of our spouse. Once we realize that none of us are perfect, and we will always evolve, we can have a greater appreciation to enjoy the time we have together. When your spouse lacks skills in a specific area, do you ever wonder why the enemy presents an outsider who seems to possess the qualities you're looking for at that time in your life? That's the 20% we discuss in the chapter titled, "Triangle Effect of Communication." It's very strategic because the flesh is never satisfied, and the small percentage of negative qualities are under a microscope.

People in successful marriages recognize these challenges. They counteract the negativity by focusing on commonality and reminding themselves about the reasons they initially said, "I do."

We must be careful not to focus on the 20% of our mate that we would like to change. A marriage unites two separate individuals, with two different upbringings and joins them as one (Genesis 2:24). Honestly, we can compromise with one another, but we won't agree with each other 100% of the time. We agree with and love 80% of our spouse, but we tend to focus on the marriage's negative aspects.

Have you heard of AstroTurf?[19] It's a factory-made product that looks like real grass. Our microwave society demands immediate ease and perfection. Societal beliefs can brainwash your thoughts and actions. Do not fool yourself into believing perfection only includes a big house, a white picket fence, two kids, and a dog. These are the benchmarks society uses to measure our relationships. Who made these things the standard of perfection? We get out of our marriage what we put into the relationship.

I asked my friend's mother what she was going to do, and she said, "Oh, I can make that grass come back." "How?" I asked.

---

[19] https://en.wikipedia.org/wiki/AstroTurf

She said, "I have some seeds in the garage that I'll spread on it. After that, I'll water it, and it'll come right back!" I looked at the grass, looked at her, shrugged my shoulders, and said, "If you say so." Four weeks later, her grass looked brand new! I couldn't believe it. "All it takes is a little work and attention. What was once dying, can live again!" she explained. From that day, I used that experience as a life principle.

Relationships have ups and downs. Some people believe the answer to their problem is a new relationship. That's not true. A new relationship only restarts the clock because your new relationship will have issues too. What if the problems are worse?

I once met a man who complained about his first wife's cooking. His second wife could cook, but she didn't enjoy sex! I'm sorry, but the second wife's issues were way more challenging than the first.

People change and mature as they age. Unfortunately, most people have trouble accepting the fact that growth and change are healthy and normal. Even wise men are not born wise. Every argument you have with your spouse is an investment in that person. You're teaching them what you want in your relationship. When you cash in your stocks before they are fully mature, you can't get upset when someone else reaps the benefits.

My mother always said, "One man's trash is another man's treasure." Please don't throw away your treasure because you think it's trash. The difference between trash and treasure is the value given to it by its owner. Someone in the world would die for your relationship. Take time to re-evaluate yours and think more about the good stuff rather than the bad.

What does this mean for your marriage? Value what you have, even if it's decaying. Your relationship takes work and routine maintenance. Like real grass, when your relationship withers, consistent care will bring it back to life.

Here are some tips to help with any withering grass in your relationship:

- **Be proactive rather than reactive.**
  - ✓ Take preventive measures and don't wait for the relationship to die.
  - ✓ Any time you seek professional help is the right time.
  - ✓ You can purchase products to prevent sprouting weeds (marital issues).
- **Maintain your grass with consistency.**
  - ✓ Date nights are essential.
  - ✓ Take some time away with one another – ALONE!
- **Keep all your equipment sharp.**
  - ✓ Talk about difficult issues in a constructive forum, even if it cuts.
  - ✓ Withering grass can be cut low and then watered regularly.
  - ✓ Focus on the positive aspects of your marriage (especially when dealing with the negative issues).
- **Lack of maintenance will allow more weeds to grow, leading to widespread damage.**
- **Even when the damage is not visible, plan for seasonal changes.**
- **Remember to enjoy the mountain top of marriages.**

# Stick – Stay – Pray

(Stick to it, Stay in it, Pray through it)

# Maintenance Prayer

Heavenly Father we thank you for today. We thank you for your unconditional love towards us. We thank you that you've allowed us to come together in holy matrimony. God, we pray right now that you would give us an open heart and mind as we read this chapter. We recognize that neither of us are perfect and we can always take the time to make improvements or adjustments. Sometimes, we fear change but give us the strength and mindset to erase all the negativity. Change is good, change shows growth - anything that doesn't grow is considered dead and anything that is dead should be buried. God, we thank you that our marriage is not dead, and we are committed to our vows. God let us not have unrealistic expectations of one another, please remind us to use the triangle effect of communication and allow you to be our filter before addressing one another. God help us to discuss our finances and the decisions we need to make for our future. God, we know Intimacy can be hard to discuss, but let us continue to have conversations with respect, love, and consideration. Father remind us that the grass isn't greener on the other side but if we continue to care for one another and put in the work - we can bring our marriage back to a healthy state. Ultimately, God we thank you that we have one another; there are so many that desire to be married so we are grateful for the blessing of consistent companionship. When it's all said and done, God remind us that all things are possible through you and that we must stick, stay and pray through any adversity that comes against what you've ordained and put together.

In Jesus name we pray.....
Amen

Stick, stay, and pray is analogous to a couple inside a building that's on fire. If both of you are in a building, or a room, without windows, doors or exits, and the room is on fire, would you choose to stay there and die, or would you try to put out the fire? Society teaches us to fend for ourselves and find the nearest exit. This is selfish, but we have been conditioned to save ourselves first. Even on a plane, the stewardess reminds us to secure our own mask before helping others. However, in marriage, God reminds us that we are one flesh *(Genesis 2:24)*. If we both worry about securing one another, we will both make it through the fire.

**STICK TO IT.** Divorce has become quite easy over the last decade. People with money have relied on prenuptial agreements for years. They are designed for the protection of assets in case you decide to end the marriage. This is the most extreme exit plan when you're entering a union intended to last a lifetime. Nowadays, you can go online and file for divorce without physically meeting with an attorney or trying to hash out any issues you have with your spouse. When you are faced with defeat, you're coached to stick to it. When you are faced with obstacles, you're coached to stick to it, and when you are faced with critical changes, you're coached to stick to it.

However, when it comes to marriage – when faced with defeat, obstacles, and critical changes – we want to quit instead of sticking to it. In any sport or competition, we are taught to complete the course and finish what we started.

STAY IN IT. When we think about defeat in marriage, the relationship has reached the irreconcilable differences phase. The definition of defeat is to win a victory over (someone) in a battle or other contest; to overcome or beat. Defeat initially begins in your mind. You start to have thoughts such as, "I can no longer do this. Maybe I made a mistake. There's no way we can recover from this issue." Think about the reasons you decided to get married, remember your vows and commitment unto God, and one another. It is easy to walk away, but it takes hard work and compromise to stay in it. [20] [21] [22] [23] There are many reasons why you should leave, and some can be justified.

---

[20] https://www.lexico.com/en/definition/defeat
[21] https://www.smudailycampus.com/sponsoredcontent/promoted/how-frequently-are-people-divorcing-in-2020
[22] https://www.insider.com/divorce-rate-changes-over-time-2019-1
[23] https://www.cdc.gov/nchs/data/dvs/national-marriage-divorce-rates-00-18.pdf

However, you need to think about the bigger picture versus your temporary issues. It is easy to rehash the problems in your marriage, but what solutions do you have to offer?

PRAY THROUGH IT. Prayer is the most underutilized weapon we have as married couples. We fight with words and keep track of faults, but we don't invest the time to take real action and wait for the proper response. We get on the phone and discuss our problems with friends and family, but we forget to take all our cares to the Lord. The bible tells us to pray without ceasing. There is always a reason to seek the counsel of God. Scripture also warns us of ungodly counsel. When was the last time you prayed with your spouse? If you can't remember, this is a great time to start. If prayer is a typical practice in your marriage, then do not stop!! In prayer, you get to hear your spouse's heart.

You get insider information about what you need to incorporate into your personal prayers. You will be surprised by the things you hear when you're talking to an unbiased power that can help the situation. Prayer works, but you will not know it until you try.

Finally, make sure your efforts are sincere and not sarcastic. It's considered a slap in the face for your spouse to improve himself or herself, based on your list, and then their efforts go unnoticed. It is essential to verbally communicate your appreciation for your spouse's effort. We easily track the negativity and throw it in each other's face, but when an attempt is made to improve the relationship, we overlook it, or we do not acknowledge it at all.

The same intense feelings you use to lay out your spouse's wrongdoings, are the same intense feelings you should use to commend your spouse's efforts.

A genuine appreciation of a conscious effort to improve goes a long way and helps build a healthy foundation. Still, we need to use the constructive criticism we receive to become better people. So, remember, along with everything else we've discussed in this book, love each other, work hard to please one another, and applaud every effort.

www.ingramcontent.com/pod-product-compliance
Lightning Source LLC
Chambersburg PA
CBHW071119090426
42736CB00012B/1950